Drinks

Contents

 **Look and put the sticker.**

water

lemonade

coffee

tea

 Put sticker on the word.

Would you like some [water] ?

Yes, please.

 Ask and say.

 Color and say.

tea

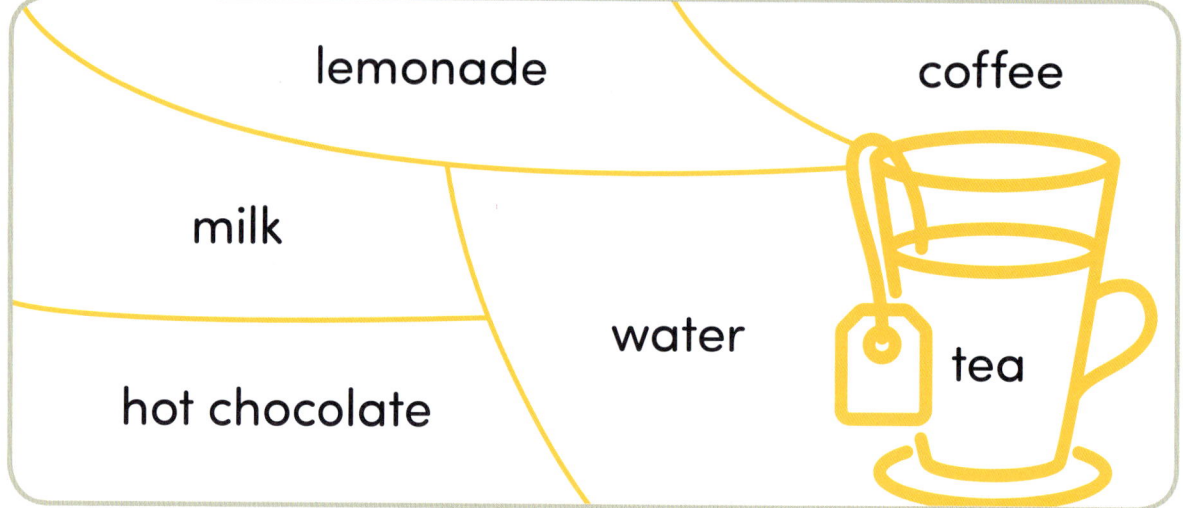

lemonade   coffee

milk

water

tea

hot chocolate

lemonade

hot chocolate

lemonade

milk

tea

orange juice

 Look and put the sticker.

milk

hot chocolate

soda

orange juice

 **Put sticker on the word.**

Would you like some milk ?

Yes, please.

 Ask and say.

p. 2

 p. 3 **water**

 p. 5

 p. 6 **milk**

Match.

milk

hot chocolate

Let's Have Fun

Sticker

Put the drinks in the machine.

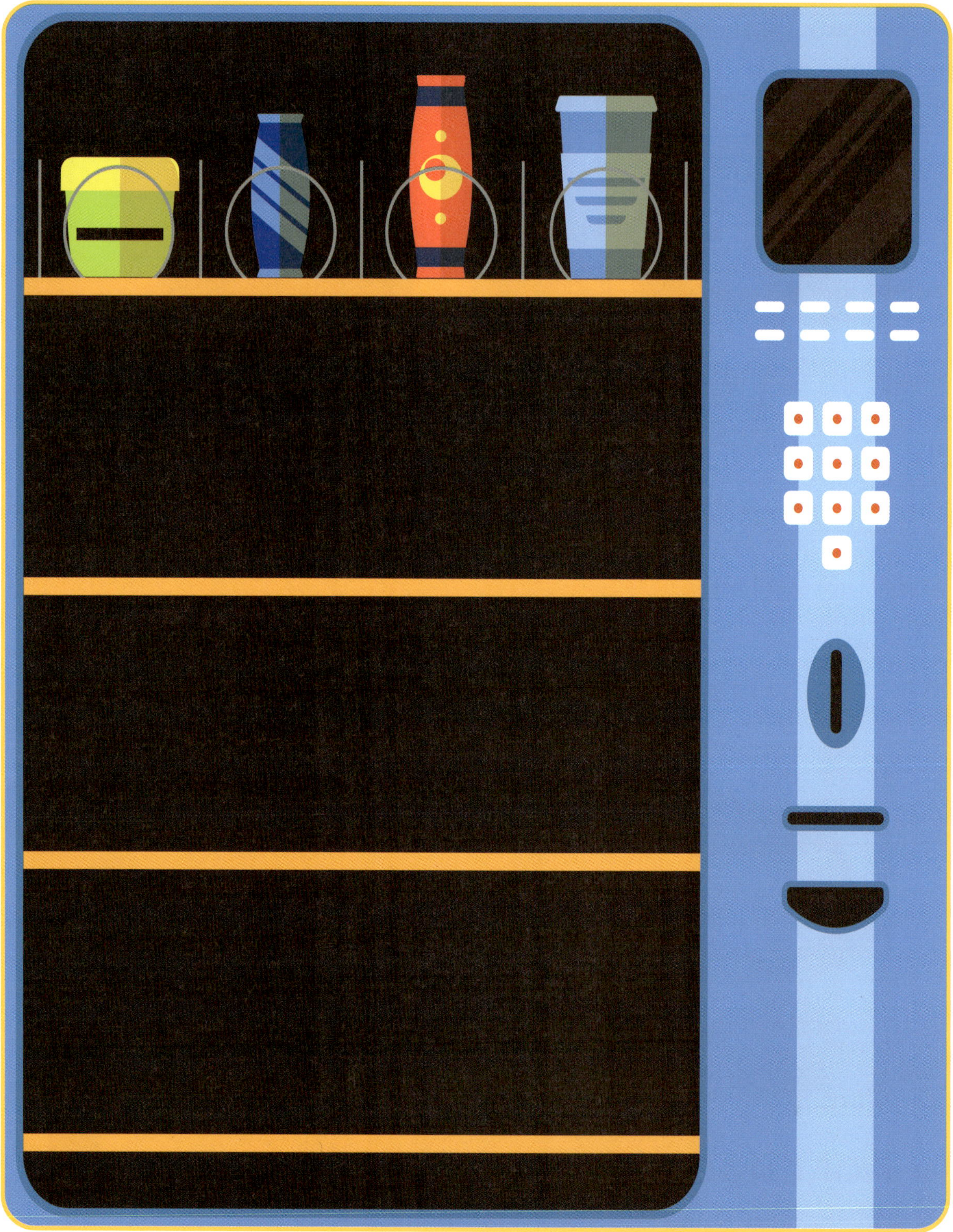

soda

water

milk

tea

orange juice

lemonade

coffee

hot chocolate